On Horsebarn Hill

On Horsebarn Hill

Poems

Janet McMillan Rives

Cover image by Blanche Serban
Author photo by Kim McNealy Sosin

ISBN: 978-1-63980-588-4

Kelsay Books
502 South 1040 East, A-119
American Fork, Utah 84003
Kelsaybooks.com

For my Storrs friends, real and imaginary

Acknowledgments

Thanks to editors of the following journals in which these poems were originally published:

The Blue Guitar: "Old Colors, New," "Twice a Cowgirl"
Fine Lines: "Mantid," "Snow Day," "I Grew Up"
Heirlock Magazine: "Starting Out"
Lyrical Iowa: "In the Attic," "Keep Searching"
MacQueen's Quinterly: "In the Dead of Winter 1944," "How to Arrange a Child's Hands"
Sandcutters: "This is the Day," "Childhood Blues"
Visions 2020: "On Horsebarn Hill"
Wingless Dreamer: "Fathers and Daughters"

My thanks to members of two poetry critique groups—Northwest Poets and Chicas Poéticas—for their sage advice over the years and to Frances Novak for her meticulous reading of this manuscript and helpful suggestions. My gratitude goes to Blanche Serban and Kim McNealy Sosin for sharing their talents of art and photography.

Contents

In the Dead of Winter 1944

after "The Birthday Interviews" by Derrick Austin

Bitter cold the day of my birth, just a week
after a Connecticut blizzard left the driveway blocked
by three feet of snow, Dad having to walk two miles
to campus, then half the class, mostly coeds,
taking the day off to go sledding down Horsebarn Hill.

The war was getting old on the day of my birth,
everyone sick of young men dying far from home,
yet no end in sight. Would the Luftwaffe bomb
the Pratt Whitney factory twenty-five miles away?
Could anyone ever stop Hitler?

Even before we came home from the hospital,
Mother was worrying about ration stamps,
never enough flour or sugar or milk these days
and now another child. Not a joyous time,
the day of my birth, but I was optimistic.

Old Colors, New

I built my studio
under the wooden ironing board
in our stark white kitchen.
The medium—Crayons,
the style—kid art.

I smelled angel food cake
cooling on a Coke bottle,
imagined twelve egg yolks
waiting to become baked custard,
chose my favorite colors:
        Prussian Blue
our New England sky.
        Indian Red, Umber, Carmine,
leaves clinging to October maples.

Colors tinted those I loved:
        Flesh
my mother's soft skin,
        Burnt Sienna
my sister's freckles,
        Cobalt Blue
my father's eyes,
        Black and White and Orange,
our cat's fur.

New colors pour
from a fresh pack.
Wild, brilliant, explosive:
        Fuchsia, Cerulean, Vivid Tangerine.
These are not comforting shades,
just reminders
of how things change.

In the Attic

When my father pulled the stairs down from the ceiling
I would climb up to the attic and gravitate
to the far end where the light of early day
reflected off dead bees strewn across the floor,
where another family's treasure gathered dust:
a rock collection glimmering in a shaft of sunlight,
butterflies pinned on white batting, their wings ablaze.

I was barely born when the fire
swept through the circus tent killing hundreds,
five from our town, two from this farmhouse.
Even when we moved a decade later,
I barely understood that our good fortune in living there
had come from others' searing sadness.

I left my stolen treasure in the attic,
left my imaginary friends, left the barn animals,
my childhood, my image of happily ever after.
Only then did I learn about change
and disenchantment, only then did I begin
to feel the heat from life's burning edge.

My Scented Childhood

winter snow
spring mud
summer sheets
line dried

leaf pile
me inside
laughter
acrid tears

hay, manure
wet horses
rotting apples
marigolds

hot lunch
creamed
chipped beef
P.U.

mimeographed
handouts
toxic
exhilarating

Mother's
Cody Emeraude
her cheek
on mine

Keep Searching

After her husband and her mother died the same year,
the year of my first birthday and her fifty-third,
my grandmother began using her railroad pass
to cross the country and visit us at our home in New England,
the second floor apartment in a farmhouse
owned by the university and surrounded by barns.
Grandmother's blindness never limited our adventures.
If she came in winter, we'd belly flop on the sled
and careen down the hill, me yelling from my perch on top:
steer, Grandma, steer, as we sailed toward the maple.
If she came in summer, we'd put a dime in an empty Chiclet box,
a yellow one, and hide it in a stone wall
on the hill up beyond the horse barn.
On her next summer visit we'd search for the dime.
We never did find the right wall or the right stone,
but we kept on hiding dimes and we kept on searching for them.
More than anything else, that's what she taught me to do.

Dairy Girls

Early mornings I'd look out the window
past our garden, beyond the cement
bull pens to the pasture where cows
waiting to be milked chewed their cuds.

At milking time, late afternoon before
dinner, before Dad came home
and scooped us up for a hug,
we'd walk up to the yellow barn.

The man doing the milking
never seemed to mind two little girls
looking over his shoulders
as he attached cups to a cow's udder.

We came home smelling of cow barn
manure with bits of straw stuck
to the bottoms of our Keds.
I marvel that Mother let us go.

This Is the Day

I am on the front porch my first day of school.
The photo is in black and white but the dress,
beautifully stitched by my mother, is dark green.
The scalloped edges of white anklets, rolled over
once, almost touch my black lace-up shoes.
I am holding a lunch pail as large as my head,
large enough to hold the baloney sandwich
and apple inside, big enough still for some crayons,
my doll, a baseball.

This is the day my life changed, the day
I walked up the hill and stood at the bus stop
where my imaginary friends hid in the stone wall.
This is the day a vivid yellow chariot
carried me away from home
and spirited me to this bright, luminous world.

Mantid

Twice we've seen him half-hidden
on a leaf near the stone wall
where my pretend friends lived
until last year when I turned seven.

Today we are the ambushers
armed with a mayonnaise jar, holes
poked in the blue lid, the bottom
lined with grass, leaves, a few beetles.

This rickety green creature,
praying at the altar of late spring,
cannot swivel his head fast enough
to see us sneak up behind him.

Captured, his five eyes stare at me
as if he understands my promise
that tomorrow, after show-and-tell
in Miss McArthur's third-grade class,

I will return him to this very spot,
place him on the back of my hand,
watch him settle into a front pew
in the church of our hillside.

Snow Day

Icy air seeps under ill-fitted windows
through which I see nothing but white—
no maple tree, no stone wall,
no church steeple, just pure white.

Bowls of corn flakes sit on our red
Chromecroft dinette table
while Mother stands at the sink,
cigarette and Coke in hand.
We listen to the Bob Steele show
on WTIC from Hartford, listen
as the Down Homers' country twang
is interrupted by a reading
of school closings: Tolland, Ashford,
Coventry, Manchester, Willimantic,
then finally, oh joy,
our Storrs Grammar School.

Hooray!
Snow day!

Fathers and Daughters

in memory of Óscar Alberto Mártinez
and his daughter, Angie Valeria

I help Dad load two inner tubes
into our 'forty-nine Ford.
We are headed to Pine Woods Pond
on this warm June Saturday.
Mother and Jamie have better things to do.
But what could be better than this?

I am still little, not a good swimmer
but I am not afraid.
Dad can swim. He helps me
learn to dog paddle.
Dad teaches me something every day,
about swimming, about words,
about telling the truth.

After we splash and kick,
stretch out on the flat rock,
talk about baseball and ice cream,
we float on our backs,
look up at the sky.

Sensory Recall

Memory is a limited archive.
—Ocean Vuong, NPR Interview, 4/5/2022

musty horse barn—oats and hay
an expanse of new-mown grass
piles of oak leaves on fire

the touch of leather—Babe's reins
in my hands, the worn grip
of a hickory-shafted five iron

the sight of jewels surround
lapis above, jade below
diamonds in the night sky

church bells every quarter hour
Mother's whistle yanking us home
blue jays announcing reveille

the first bite of yellow cake
made from scratch, wild
blackberries, coffee ice cream

Childhood Blues

Baby blue, threadbare now, once
silky edge of a towel my mother
could not throw away, so tonight
this fabric that once wrapped me
will cover lobelia as the desert freezes.

UConn blue, not quite navy,
on tee shirts, pennants, beanies,
but especially on a cardboard cup
holding ice cream made by a dairy
science major, an A-student I hoped.

Bicycle blue, like every girl's three speed
in the fifties, bought with the savings bond
my grandparents gave me at birth,
cashed in for my independence.

So many childhood blues live on,
but those I hold closest are two:
the cobalt waves in my mother's eyes,
the steel beams in my father's.

On Horsebarn Hill

At nine I knew what happy meant—
the opposite of bustling, the slow pace
of a one-stop-light town, even slower
on the edge, no neighbors, just four of us
each finding our way in a rented farmhouse

horses nickering their joy
in the riding ring next door, cows
mooing, chewing in the pasture,
pigs, an oink, a squeal, a grunt

the red barn up the hill, the bluest
summer sky, a blinding yellow sun,
then blue mixed with yellow making
green everywhere—maples, pines,
hills, ivy trellised wallpaper,
two-toned Ford, mint and evergreen,
out back Mother's glads bursting
into every vibrant shade of gold,
orange, purple, burgundy

pot roast in the oven, angel food cake
cooling on the kitchen table, carrots
straight from the garden, ice cream
for ten cents fresh from the college dairy.

At nine I knew what happy meant
yet how strange to find it today—quiet
moments in self quarantine, sounds of birds,
wind, the scent of rain, a world alive—
unexpected gifts of human isolation.

Starting Out

I would start out at the top of the hill
and survey the scene of my beginnings.
I would place a protractor on this map
of memories and measure the angles,
the degrees of my comings and goings
no more than a thousand steps from start to finish.
In the middle, along the straight edge,
I'd find the house of my childhood
so much bigger than any I've seen since
I'm afraid to think how tiny it might have been.

In the horse barn I'd find the blue-veined wooden horse
I'd have been afraid to learn from
and those two gentle souls, Babe and Andy,
slow enough for even me to ride.
I'd wander down the hill to the cow barn,
let the bulls scare me, watch the cows be milked
and spend my dime on a tub of ice cream
eaten with a wooden spoon and shared
with my stonewall friends, more real to me
than the flesh and blood kids who came to play.

The semicircle I'd trace would hold our two maples,
one for show and one for play—
that one I'd climb to where the robins lived.
After I had examined the nest,
every twig, every piece of straw,
I would start out into the world
and begin to learn about life.

Etched in Leather

For exciting new beauty . . . custom-built hand-made occasional
tables with gold tooled leather tops banded with highlighting inlays.
Regularly 3 for 149.85. Can be purchased separately.
          —Ad in *The Hartford Times,* 1950

Our living room became fancier
with each purchase—a wing-back chair
in gold print, a traditional couch
in lovely green damask, matching chair
in green and gold stripes.

A photo shows Jamie and me snuggling
in the wing-back, flipping through pages
of *The Night before Christmas.*
I was allowed to sit on the couch
especially after we bought a TV
housed in a tall mahogany console.

I remember all the furniture
in that rather formal living room
especially the rectangular end table,
part of a set of three, the table
where on a late spring Saturday
in nineteen-fifty-one, the end of first grade,
I placed a sheet of double-lined paper
on top, leaned over slightly,
and carefully printed my name
        Janet Ann McMillan
forever etched in leather.

Horsebarn Hill: Two Views

for Blanche Serban

You gather paints, easel,
canvas, pack your car
for the drive across town
set up your outdoor studio
at the base of the hill.

                I hop off the porch
                skip past the riding ring
                climb over a wall
                of unmortared stone
                beside the red barn.

You find the deepest green
for the hedgerow, strong
mustard yellow to capture
the sunlit hillside, flecks
of mauve in two scruffy trees.

                On a day not meant
                for lessons, I embrace
                the chestnut mare
                my tiny hand on her neck
                a sweet smell of new hay.

You add billowing clouds
touches of lemon and rose
floating below an azure
sky too massive
for me to ever forget.

On Horseback

in memory of Jamie Lynn McMillan

She was older, the leader, smart, the reader, skilled,
the equestrian. Perched on a spirited horse,
hands exquisitely holding the reins, she exuded
confidence, control. I hung on the rails watching,
admiring. When I was old enough, about four,
Jamie got us up, dressed, fed and on our way
to the red barn on top of the hill.

They gave Babe to me, the biggest horse given
to the smallest kid. I should say they gave me to Babe,
my caretaker, gentle enough to calm even the most shy
scaredy-cat. Babe with her enormous chestnut buttocks,
me on top, feet barely reaching beyond the saddle,
Jamie eyeing me, checking on her little sister.

A few years later I rode Andy, retired U.S. Cavalry,
black mane clipped short, neck branded.
Andy didn't need any more action. He was content
to carry me around the ring, never more than
a brisk trot, nothing to alarm a kid who was clearly
unhappy on a horse, who wanted to be at home
playing ball or writing stories.

Yet there I was each Saturday
willing to go horseback riding to please my parents
but mostly to watch my sister
shine in the circle of her light.

After the Farmhouse

Before, I was mostly alone
or with my sister or parents.
After, neighbors were everywhere,
friends in our yards, our houses.

Before, the sky meant everything to me,
two thirds of what I saw each day.
After, trees filled my space,
leaves and birds of every color.

Before, a bus took me to school
with kids I barely knew.
After, I walked with best friends
through our woods, our nature.

Before, I was protected by isolation,
by family, by a church spire.
After, the world was mine to discover
on a girl's blue three-speed.

Before, I wrote little stories filled
with misspellings, presents for Mother.
After, more stories and poems, too,
gifts to myself.

How to Arrange a Child's Hands

Mother placed my fingers
on the Underwood's home row
index fingers on F and J.
Hover your thumbs over the space bar
she told me *wrists raised, eyes up.*

Dad set the grip of a cut-down
golf club onto my left palm
placed my right hand on top. *Hold it*
gently he said *like a baby bird.*

Addie boosted me onto Babe's saddle
threaded the reins around my fingers.
Make a fist she instructed *press the thumbs*
straight down against the leather.

Jamie, big sister, laced my fingers
tips down index fingers and thumbs up.
Here is the church, here is the steeple
thumbs flew apart, hands flipped
open the doors and see all the people.

See all the people, their faces.
Hear all the people, their voices.

Dinner Table Etiquette

We kept our places, Dad at one end
Mother at the other close to the kitchen
me on the side to her left, his right
my skinny sister across from me
pushing food around her plate
while teaching us new vocabulary words.

And when we moved across town
we still kept our places
Mother sharing neighborhood gossip
Jamie news from school
Dad and I exchanging a subtle glance
always staying quiet.

My Natural History

Hills, fields, scent of manure,
Holsteins, Morgan mares,
stacks of hay, sacks of oats.
A search for birds' nests,
daddy-longlegs, dandelions,
pale blue robins' eggs,
beetles picked off gladiolus,
dropped into jars of oily water.
Chasing squirrels, climbing
stone walls, split-rail fences,
bronze maples. A small body
captured by an evening
snowfall, above me
stars.

Groves of white pines
hiding frozen ponds, tangy
winter berries. My fingers
stuck to ice-laden twigs, dipped
into half-hidden brooks, mud,
rubbed across mossy rocks,
laced around stems of pink
lady slippers. Acorns, pinecones
crunching under my feet,
blue jays jeering, a dogwood's
five perfect petals. The warmth
of mown grass, itch of poison ivy,
pungent odor of leaves
burning.

Homecoming

A tiny house on Wormwood Hill
       still there
the young family of four
crowded onto a single Adirondack chair
posing, all smiles.

A farmhouse next to the college barns
       still there
the house I mean, not the barns
and Mother at the kitchen window
watching her children at play.

A stucco bungalow at 707 North Euclid
       still there
guarded by a wall of black
volcanic rock from *A Mountain*
Grandma hanging clothes out back.

A gray split level on Eastwood Road
       still there
pink flowering dogwoods
blooming left and right
Dad leaning on the lawnmower.

       Still there
all of my childhood houses
peopled forever by family ghosts.

I Grew Up

Outside:
almost always,
save for blizzard and hurricane.

In the woods:
walking to school,
heading to a friend's house.

On my own:
in the sandbox,
cruising on my bike.

With friends:
first imaginary,
then real live neighbors.

Of a family:
setting the table,
sweeping, Saturday chores.

I grew up
playing,
writing, walking,
reading, thinking, talking.

Just as today.

What I Learned on Horsebarn Hill

I learned to walk   talk   share
    I'll cut   you choose
to draw   sing   play

I learned when roosters wake
cows are milked
the school bus comes

when Mother's tired
    please girls

when Dad's not joking
    I'm going to count to ten

I learned to tie my shoes
climb the maple

ride a two-wheeler
    look mom   no hands

throw a baseball
love a cat

I learned these lessons
on Horsebarn Hill
stored them up for now

Rules for Removing a Black Mark

after "Weight" by John Freeman

Mother warned me not to lie
      or hurt others
      or think only of myself.
Each bad act, she said,
      would mean another black
      mark on my heart
leaving it, well before pleated skirts
      and saddle shoes, a charred
      shriveled piece of coal.

What Mother forgot to say
      or perhaps could not have known
      at her young age
was that I might become wise
      with the passage of time
      more tender, more caring
until each black bruise
      would fade, revealing
      a rosy heart restored.

The Turning

Each afternoon at 4:30, the whistle sounded.
It could be heard from one end of campus
to the other, centered as it was in the power plant
just beyond the lake.

The whistle was meant for the university's
hourly workers—men who managed heating
systems, cleaned classrooms, women
who worked as secretaries or cooked
in dining halls.

But all of us lived by the 4:30 whistle.

That piercing sound marked the point
when we turned from connections
with outsiders—co-workers, friends—
to intimate insiders, our families.
At the dinner table, each of us recounted
our daily miracles. After was the time
to relax, read, draw pictures.

No whistle for me these days
no colleagues, no students to leave behind.
Yet inside me a whistle blows. It's 4:30.
I turn to feed the dog, watch the news,
idle my motor, reflect.

Embedded Memory

Do I miss apples gathered
from where they fell in the orchard?

The acrid odor of burning leaves?

A sense of ice between my toes
on a skating day?

Do I mourn the cat once curled beside my hip?

Rain tapping on the window
turning to ice as it falls on a cold day?

Do I long for blue birds—jays and warblers

for raspberries picked in the woods
lady slippers, dogwoods, maples?

Yes, all of these I remember

store them on a high shelf
in the bedroom closet

retrieve them on a lonely day.

My Last Lesson on Horsebarn Hill

Seven years after we'd moved
from that rented house
from the maples and pines

on a quiet Sunday afternoon
the spring of my sixteenth year
my father drove to Horsebarn Hill

to the back side
empty of people and cars
just the pigs getting muddy
in their new digs.

With me behind the wheel
of our Renault Dauphine
he taught me how to drive
how to press the clutch
with my left foot

and gently slide
into first gear.

Twice a Cowgirl

That was the year I ate alone almost every Saturday,
listened to KTKT on my unwieldy portable,
used my clothes allowance to buy Levi 501s,
turquoise western shirt, white cowboy belt
with a huge silver buckle. That was the year
I turned seventeen, the year we moved west,
traded our maple syrup for prickly pear jelly.

I thought western clothes might turn me into
a happy teenager, might make me feel like I did
ten years earlier, on my seventh birthday,
no doubt a frigid February in New England.
In the dog-eared photo taken that day,
my jacket hangs on the porch railing—no way
I'd cover up the plaid shirt with pearl buttons,
red bandana tied around my neck,
rabbit's foot suspended from a belt loop
on my jeans, me smiling a lost-baby-tooth grin
on that my lucky day.

By seventeen I was ten years and twenty-five
hundred miles from that tiny cowgirl in the photo,
a teenager now, dressed not just for a birthday party
but for the entire rodeo week in Tucson
including two days off from school
to watch barrel racers, bull riders, calf ropers.
What made me think looking like a cowgirl
could bring back the joy of childhood?
The tooth fairy had long ago filled the gap
in my smile, but other pieces were missing—
a sister gone off to college, parents out again
at some fund-raiser, my friends of a lifetime
back east, sledding the hills of my homeplace.

An Introduction to Music and Literature

We had plenty of books
       The Night before Christmas
       cut in the shape of Santa on a sled
       Heidi with her grandfather and Peter
       One Hundred and One Famous Poems
and so many Golden Books
       Scruffy the Tugboat
       The Circus Is in Town
       The Little Engine that Could.

Later came biographies with orange covers
       Molly Pitcher Girl Patriot
       George Washington Boy Leader
books we'd check out from the library
in Mansfield Center, no doubt the reason
I'm the one to suggest memoirs
for my senior women's book club
       Brown Girl Dreaming
       The Home Place.

We owned two 78 rpm records
       Prokofiev's Peter and the Wolf
played on Sunday afternoons
orchestral instruments setting me to wonder
what else might be in store for me
later in my life
       Yo Yo Ma performing Bach
       Andre Previn and the Pittsburgh Symphony.

Our second phonograph record
       Tex Ritter's Big Rock Candy Mountain
left a beat in my soul, a western twang
that later led me to join in from the audience
as Vince Gill sang his classics on an Iowa stage.

Helicopter Parents

            three adults
        sitting on a bench one June day
            my parents   mid-fifties
me twenty-seven   a working girl

three of us with maple-tree helicopters
                stuck on our noses
            seed pods when pulled apart
a surface as sticky as glue

        we took flight in laughter

me teaching them a kid's trick
            I'd learned on Horsebarn Hill
                    in the shadow of our maples

                my parents
always of the free range ilk
            raised us as they'd been raised
                rules   yes
        be prompt   polite   truthful
but few boundaries to constrain us

        they did not hover

until on that one summer day
            with odd devices stuck on their noses
I finally saw them as they were
            my helicopter parents

Guardian

of memories from Horsebarn Hill

three red-handled kitchen tools
mesh strainer   slotted spoon
          melon scoop   summer picnics

linen tea towel   worn soft
turquoise image of San Xavier Mission
          sacred pilgrimage

orange ceramic bowl
scalloped edge
          to celebrate a wedding

photo of me   red shirt   wry smile
breathing out five candles
          my birthday

watercolor in greens   Yugoslavian
farm scene   bought for $5
          the year I was born

The Stars We Once Were

. . . we begin to understand how we are each many people,
including the stars we once were . . .
     —Linda Hogan, "Hearing Voices"

Remember how we stood under the maple
one starry June night, our little family
holding hands? You and Mother
tried to surprise and enchant us
with stories of things that happened
before we came to Horsebarn Hill,
before we were even born.

We know! We know!
We were watching.
We were stars in the sky.
We saw it all.

Now on this cool clear night,
summer's shortest,
I survey the stars that surround me
and wonder which one is you.

What to Claim

And who wouldn't want again . . .
  —Jenny George, "Migration"

I'd want the young father
letting go of the rear wheel
watching the girl fly down the hill
on her big sister's bike

and the young mother
telling her child she could wear anything
she wanted to her fifth birthday party—
Levi's, boots, flannel shirt.

The robins wedged among branches
of the silver maple—I'd claim them too
and the sister holding a tiny hand
as we walk to the school bus stop.

I'd capture aromas from the kitchen—
pot roast, gingerbread, bacon
and even stinky smells—cows,
horses, pigs, all that manure.

Mostly I'd gather days of energy,
freedom, warmth, years when I was
part of the clutch, helping build a nest
with those I loved.

About the Author

Janet McMillan Rives was born and raised in Storrs, Connecticut and moved to Tucson, Arizona as a teenager. She is a graduate of the University of Arizona and Duke University. After retiring as a professor of economics from the University of Northern Iowa, she moved to her current residence in Oro Valley, Arizona. When not busy with poetry, Janet enjoys golf, gardening, and the company of her dog. Her poems have appeared in such journals as *Raw Art Review, Ekphrastic Review, Beyond Words, Book of Matches, Sandcutters, Crosswinds, Creosote,* and *Canary,* as well as in a number of anthologies. She has published three chapbooks: *Into This Sea of Green: Poems from the Prairie* (Finishing Line Press, 2020), *Washed by a Summer Rain: Poems from the Desert* (Kelsay Books, 2023), and *Thread: A Memoir in Woven Poems* (Finishing Line Press, 2024).

www.ingramcontent.com/pod-product-compliance
Lightning Source LLC
Chambersburg PA
CBHW030815090426
42737CB00010B/1280